HAL•LEONARD
INSTRUMENTAL PLAY-ALONG

AUDIO ACCESS INCLUDED

TENOR SAX

JAMES BOND

PLAYBACK+
Speed • Pitch • Balance • Loop

To access audio visit:
www.halleonard.com/mylibrary

Enter Code
6753-5154-6497-0510

Audio arrangements by Peter Deneff

ISBN 978-1-4950-6081-6

𝄞 Music Sales America

EXCLUSIVELY DISTRIBUTED BY

HAL•LEONARD®

7777 W. BLUEMOUND RD. P.O. BOX 13819 MILWAUKEE, WI 53213

Visit Hal Leonard Online at
www.halleonard.com

DIAMONDS ARE FOREVER

from DIAMONDS ARE FOREVER

TENOR SAX

Words by DON BLACK
Music by JOHN BARRY

FOR YOUR EYES ONLY

from FOR YOUR EYES ONLY

TENOR SAX

Lyrics by MICHAEL LESSON
Music by BILL CONTI

FROM RUSSIA WITH LOVE

from FROM RUSSIA WITH LOVE

TENOR SAX

Words and Music by
LIONEL BART

GOLDFINGER
from GOLDFINGER

TENOR SAX

Music by JOHN BARRY
Lyrics by LESLIE BRICUSSE and ANTHONY NEWLEY

JAMES BOND THEME

TENOR SAX

By MONTY NORMAN

LIVE AND LET DIE

from LIVE AND LET DIE

TENOR SAX

Words and Music by PAUL McCARTNEY
and LINDA McCARTNEY

NOBODY DOES IT BETTER

from THE SPY WHO LOVED ME

TENOR SAX

Music by MARVIN HAMLISCH
Lyrics by CAROLE BAYER SAGER

ON HER MAJESTY'S SECRET SERVICE - THEME

TENOR SAX

By JOHN BARRY

SKYFALL

from the Motion Picture SKYFALL

TENOR SAX

Words and Music by ADELE ADKINS
and PAUL EPWORTH

Slowly, with feeling

A VIEW TO A KILL

from A VIEW TO A KILL

TENOR SAX

Words and Music by JOHN BARRY
and DURAN DURAN

WRITING'S ON THE WALL

from the film SPECTRE

TENOR SAX

Words and Music by SAM SMITH
and JAMES NAPIER

YOU ONLY LIVE TWICE

from YOU ONLY LIVE TWICE

TENOR SAX

Music by JOHN BARRY
Lyrics by LESLIE BRICUSSE